MW01026583

SECRETS OF ADULTHOOD

SECRETS OF
ADULTHOOD

Simple Truths for
Our Complex Lives

GRETCHEN RUBIN

CROWN
NEW YORK

CROWN
An imprint of the Crown Publishing Group
A division of Penguin Random House LLC
1745 Broadway
New York, NY 10019
crownpublishing.com
penguinrandomhouse.com

Line art by Shutterstock.com/kawsar_moblu

The Library of Congress catalog record is available at
https://lccn.loc.gov/2024028887.

Hardcover ISBN 978-0-593-80073-7
Ebook ISBN 978-0-593-80074-4

Editor: Gillian Blake
Editorial assistants: Amy Li / Jessica Scott
Production editor: Christine Tanigawa
Text designer: Andrea Lau
Production manager: Heather Williamson

Manufactured in the United States of America

1st Printing

First Edition

The authorized representative in the EU for product safety and
compliance is Penguin Random House Ireland, Morrison Chambers,
32 Nassau Street, Dublin D02 YH68, Ireland,
https://eu-contact.penguin.ie.

To Eliza and Eleanor . . . everyday life in Utopia

CONTENTS

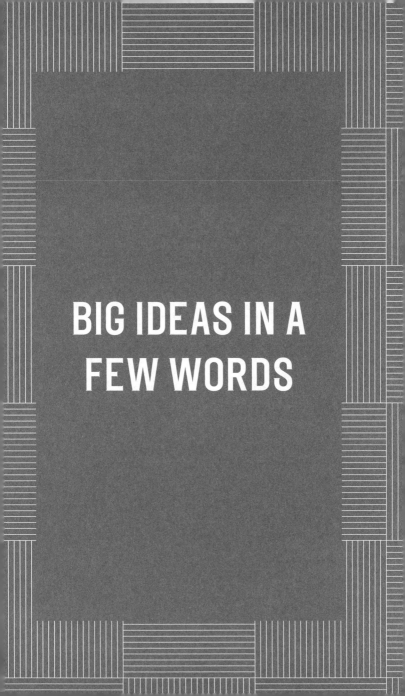

BIG IDEAS IN A FEW WORDS

With time and experience, life teaches us lessons—usually the hard way.

As my two daughters were growing up, I wanted to share the "Secrets of Adulthood" I'd learned, to save them from repeating the mistakes I had made. Some of these insights I'd gained through my own experiences, others I'd gleaned from reflecting on the experiences of others.

But even more than sharing my knowledge with my daughters, I wanted to remind myself of what I'd learned. All too often, I found myself rediscovering the same lessons, over and over. How many times have I thought, "Gretchen, *remember,* working is one of the most dangerous forms of procrastination."

I realized that I needed a collection of these secrets just as much as my daughters did, and I began to keep a list. What Secrets of Adulthood did I use to help me tackle a difficult decision? Or to fight temptation, or calm down, or know myself better? Or to change myself, when I wanted to change?

As this list began to grow, I challenged myself to shape these secrets into the form of the aphorism.

For my whole life, I've loved the literary form of the aphorism. An *aphorism* is a concise statement that contains an expansive truth. Unlike the folk wisdom of proverbs—"A stumble may prevent a fall" or "You can't push a rope"—aphorisms can be attributed to a particular person.

Brief and sharp, aphorisms distill big ideas into few words; by saying little, they manage to suggest more. The clarity of their language promotes the clarity of our thinking.

As a child, I collected aphorisms in my "blank books"—books with blank pages that I filled with quotations illustrated by magazine cuttings. Once I became a writer exploring human nature, my admiration for the form grew, because human nature is the chief subject of the greatest aphorists. In my own work, I explore how we can make our lives happier, healthier, more productive, and more creative, and all the great aphorists tackle those questions. (My first book was *Power Money Fame Sex,* and the aphorists certainly cover those subjects!)

Over and over, I've found that the right aphorism, invoked at the right time, can help me manage the complexities of life. For instance, when I was trying to decide whether my family should get a dog, the pros and cons lists seemed to be equally balanced, and I couldn't make up my mind. Finally I remembered, "Choose the bigger life"—and the decision became easy. We got a dog.

Because of my respect for aphorisms, I'm always searching for more. My bookshelves are crowded with masterpieces of philosophy and literature that are largely collections of aphorisms, such as Confucius's *Analects,* Lao-tzu's *Tao-te Ching,* Marcus Aurelius's *Meditations,* Blaise Pascal's *Pensées,* and Georg Christoph Lichtenberg's *The Waste Books.* Some of my favorite writers who excel in aphorisms include Michel de Montaigne, Joseph Joubert, James Baldwin, Heraclitus, Jules Renard, Nicolas Chamfort, William Edward Hartpole Lecky, Oscar Wilde, Warren Buffett, G. K. Chesterton, William Hazlitt, Zora Neale Hurston, Ralph Waldo Emerson, and George Orwell. Over the years, I've collected hundreds of my favorite aphorisms.

Marie von Ebner-Eschenbach is one of the aphorists I admire most: "You can sink so fast that you think you're flying." Another is François de La Rochefoucauld: "It is much easier to stifle a first desire than to gratify all those that follow it." Samuel Johnson's aphoristic style is one reason that I read and re-read his essays: "All severity that does not tend to increase good, or prevent evil, is idle." People might not expect fiction to be a particularly rich source of aphorisms, but many of my favorites come from novels. Consider Iris Murdoch's "Curiosity is not the same thing as a thirst for knowledge." Andy Warhol's art doesn't interest me much, but I collect his surprising, gnomic observations: "Nobody really looks at anything; it's too hard." My favorite contemporary aphorist is Sarah Manguso: "Failure is good preparation for success, which comes as a pleasant surprise, but success is poor preparation for failure." And, of course, there's Winston Churchill: "To be really happy and really safe, one ought to have at least two or three hobbies, and they must all be real."

These days, the aphorism is a mostly neglected art—though sometimes it pops up in its lesser forms, like the self-improvement cliché on social media or the office poster's reminder about the value of teamwork. This ancient discipline, however, still has tremendous power to communicate.

Because aphorisms are short and well-expressed, they're easy to remember and have more vigor in the mind.

Because we must decide whether we agree or disagree, aphorisms provoke our reflection. We can also compare how different aphorists express a similar idea, as they often do, or contemplate how they contradict each other. For instance, Publilius Syrus observed, "No man is happy who does not think himself so," while Vauvenargues wrote, "There are men who are happy without knowing it."

The discipline of the aphorism forces precision of thinking. In my own writing, I've found that I can express a big idea in a few words only if I truly understand what I'm trying to say. And, as demonstrated by the haiku, the sonnet, and the thirty-minute sitcom, imagination is often better served by constraint than by freedom.

For the reader, then, fewer words supply greater wisdom; for the aphorist, brevity sparks creativity. So, the more I study happiness and human nature, and the longer I live, the more I challenge myself to distill what I learn into brief, memorable aphorisms: "Accept yourself, and expect more from yourself," "No tool fits every hand," "We care for many people we don't particularly care for."

After years of adding, subtracting, and polishing, I've written my own giant trove, from which this collection has been selected. For *Secrets of Adulthood*, I've weeded out any aphorism that is a mere observation, such as "The tulip is an empty flower" or "The Periodic Table of the Elements is an ingredient list of the universe." (Well, I have to admit, I couldn't resist including a *few* of these observations.) I've also omitted my large set of bleak aphorisms, which make for discouraging reading. Here, I've included those secrets that I hope will help others navigate adulthood—both people who are just entering adulthood and also people who, like me, are often surprised to realize, "Yikes, I'm a grown-up. What now?" Sometimes, a single sentence can provide all the insight we need.

A few notes: While the mic-drop quality is a big part of the aphorism's appeal, some do benefit from more discussion. So here, alongside the formal aphorisms, I've sometimes added a few brief illustrative stories.

Also, as I was writing my Secrets of Adulthood, I kept adding to a different list—practical hacks that, I've discovered, make day-to-day life easier. Does "If you can't find something, clean up" express a deep truth about human nature? Maybe not. But it's still a useful thing to remember, so in the final section, "Simple Secrets of Adulthood," I've included a collection of those minor secrets.

What a joy it has been to work on my Secrets of Adulthood, to distill my observations and experiences into general truths! After all, work is the play of adulthood.

CULTIVATING OURSELVES

Because I write about human nature, people sometimes say to me, "Give me the short answer. What's the best, the most scientifically proven way to become happier?" (Or healthier, or more productive, or more creative.)

"Well, there's no one best way," I respond. "We each have to figure it out for ourselves."

"Sure, sure," they agree. "Just tell me the *best* way."

For a long time, this question stumped me, but now when people ask, "What's the best way to create a happy life?" I respond, "What's the best way to cook an egg?" Puzzled, they respond, "Well, it depends on how you like your eggs." I answer, "Exactly! We each have the answer that's right for *us*."

Because we're all different, there can't be a one-size-fits-all answer to tell us how to achieve our aims. Other people can suggest possibilities, but they can't figure it out for us—and we can't figure it out for them. Self-knowledge is key, because we can build a happy life only on the foundation of our own values, interests, strengths, and temperament.

And yet it's hard to know ourselves. It's easy to assume, "Of course I know myself, I just hang out with myself all day long." In fact, distracted by the way we *wish* we were, or by what we *think* we ought to be, or by what others *assume* we are, we lose sight of what's actually true. But when we know ourselves, we can shape our lives to reflect our own nature and values.

Here are some Secrets of Adulthood that I learned the hard way.

THE PROJECT
OF HAPPINESS

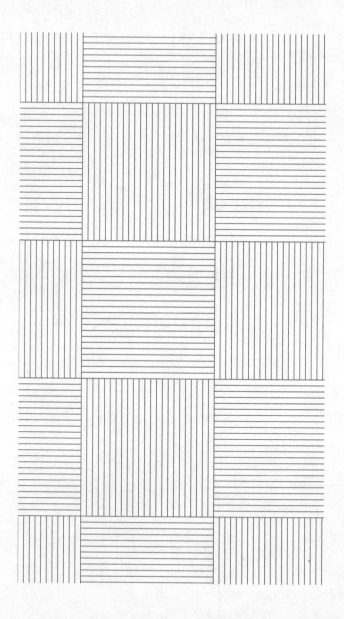

Happiness doesn't always make us feel happy.

Living up to our values, challenging ourselves, facing our mistakes, depriving ourselves . . . these aims make our lives happier, but they don't always make us feel happy in the moment.

———

One of the best ways to make *yourself* happy is to make *others* happy.

One of the best ways to make *others* happy is to be happy *yourself.*

———

There is no right way to create a happier life, just as there is no best way to cook an egg.

———

Be selfish, if only for selfless reasons; be selfless, if only for selfish reasons.

—

Nothing takes us out of ourselves more than being of use.

—

It's hard to be happy if we're not happy at home; it's hard to be happy if we're not happy at work.

—

Sometimes we can minister to the body through the spirit; sometimes we can minister to the spirit through the body.

SELF-IMPROVEMENT

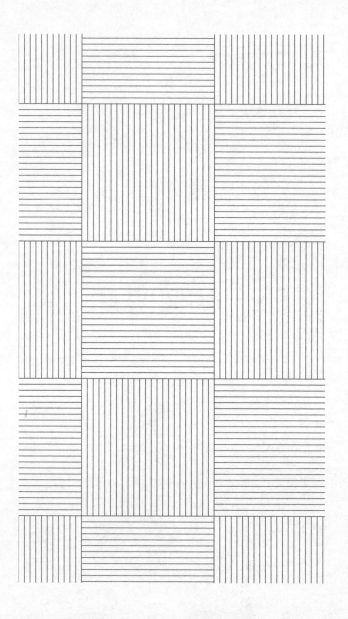

Sometimes, to change our habits we must change our identity.

At a young age, writer James Agee had serious heart trouble, and his doctors told him that he needed to cut back on drinking and smoking. He wrote to a friend:

> I am depressed because whether I am to live a very short time or relatively longer time depends . . . on whether or not I can learn to be the kind of person I am not and have always detested.

And indeed, Agee didn't cut back on the drinking and smoking, and he died of a heart attack, at age forty-five, in a taxi on his way to see a doctor. To change his habits, he would have had to become the kind of person he'd always detested. No wonder it was hard for him to change.

When we recognize a clash between the identity we have and the change we seek, we can decide whether that identity still reflects our true values.

—

There is no magic, one-size-fits-all solution to happiness or good habits.

—

Accept yourself, and expect more from yourself.

—

Good intentions mean nothing unless they inspire practical actions.

—

What we do *every day* matters more than what we do *once in a while*.

—

It's easier to change our surroundings and our schedules than to change ourselves.

—

Don't expect to be motivated by motivation.

—

We can all arrive at the same destination, but we may get there by different roads.

—

Habits are the invisible architecture of everyday life; we can change our lives by changing our habits.

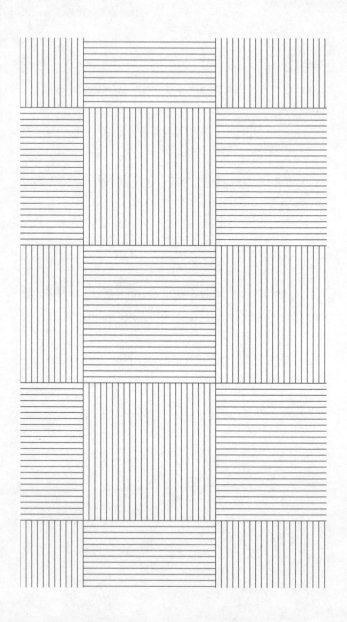

COMFORT

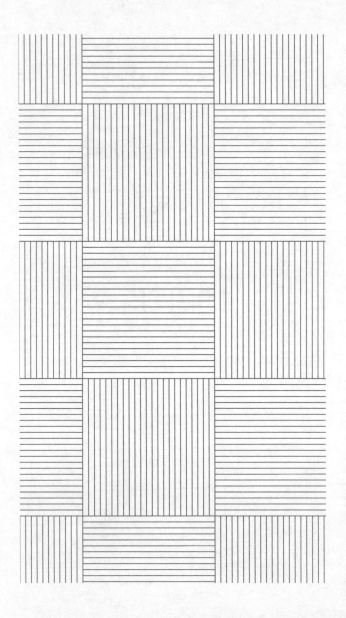

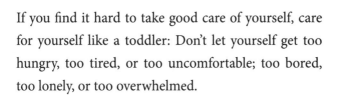

If you find it hard to take good care of yourself, care for yourself like a toddler: Don't let yourself get too hungry, too tired, or too uncomfortable; too bored, too lonely, or too overwhelmed.

—

People don't talk enough about how *comforting* work is.

—

To make solitude more pleasant, add a quiet, wordless presence: a candle flame, a flower in a vase, a fish swimming in a bowl.

—

Recognize that, like sleeping with a big dog in a small bed, things that are uncomfortable can also be comforting.

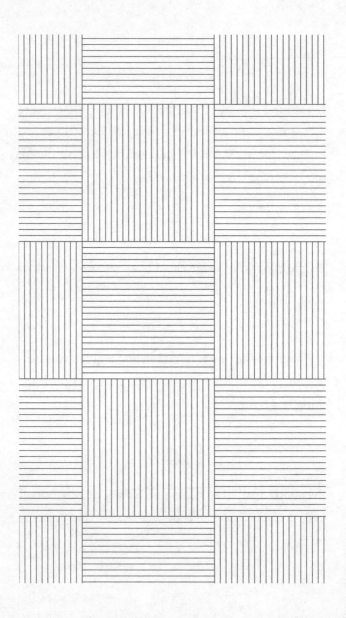

SELF-REALIZATION

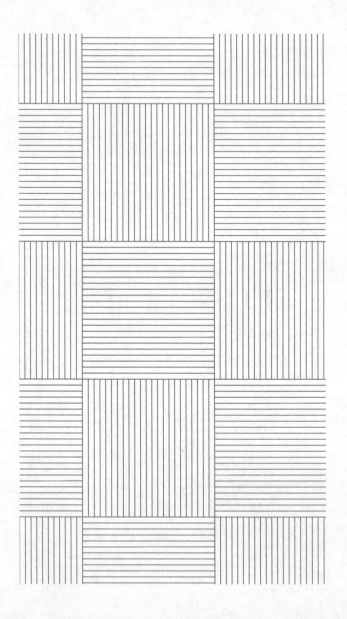

Character isn't what we hope to be or do, or intend to be or do; it's what we actually *do*, when given a choice. Nevertheless, we often argue that it's not fair to judge us by our behavior. A doctor said, "I have a great bedside manner, I just never use it." Lawyer Michael Cohen said, "I have lied, but I am not a liar. I have done bad things, but I am not a bad man." Notorious murderer Malcolm Macarthur didn't consider himself to be the type of person to be a murderer.

———

We're often better off admitting uncomfortable facts about ourselves rather than trying to disguise them. Nebraska saw great success with its tourist slogan, "Honestly, it's not for everyone." Marmite, the yeast-based savory food spread, declared, "You either love it or you hate it."

———

The traffic changes, the weather changes, yet the same people are always late, and the same people are always on time.

———

We can change our lives without changing ourselves.

———

We know if something is important to us if it shows up in our schedule, our spending, and our space.

———

We should pay special attention to anything that we lie about, or try to hide.

———

The bird, the bee, and the bat all fly, but they use different kinds of wings.

———

Are you painting your own fakes?

There's a story about an art dealer who bought a canvas signed "Picasso." To verify its authenticity, he visited Picasso at the artist's Cannes studio. After a glance at the painting, Picasso declared, "It's a fake."

Just a few months later, the dealer returned with another "Picasso." He returned to Cannes, showed it to Picasso, and Picasso dismissed it as a fake.

"But, *cher maître,*" said the dealer, "it so happens that I saw you with my own eyes working on this very picture several years ago."

Picasso replied, "I often paint fakes."

Sometimes, we paint our own fakes—and we should try to recognize it, when we do.

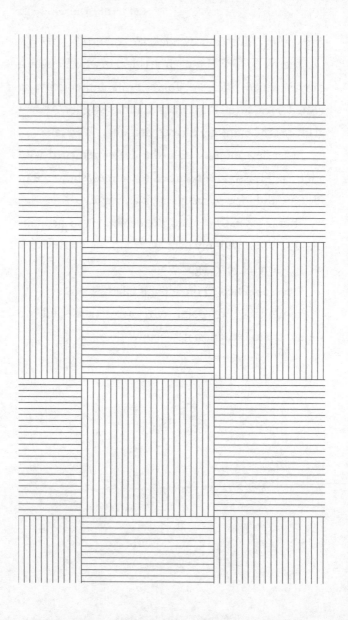

ADVENTURE

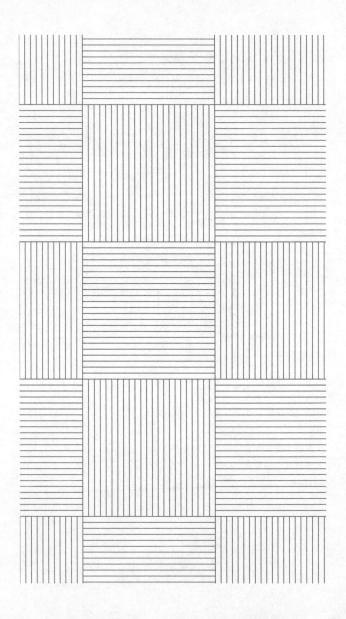

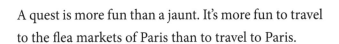

A quest is more fun than a jaunt. It's more fun to travel to the flea markets of Paris than to travel to Paris.

—

Pay the tourist tax. Getting cheated occasionally is a small price to pay for trusting others.

—

The world looks different from a footpath than from a car.

—

What's fun for other people may not be fun for you, and vice versa.

—

The pilgrim and the tourist visit the same shrine, but they find something different.

—

Much of the appeal of an ice-cream truck comes from the fact that we're never sure when it will appear.

MEMORIES

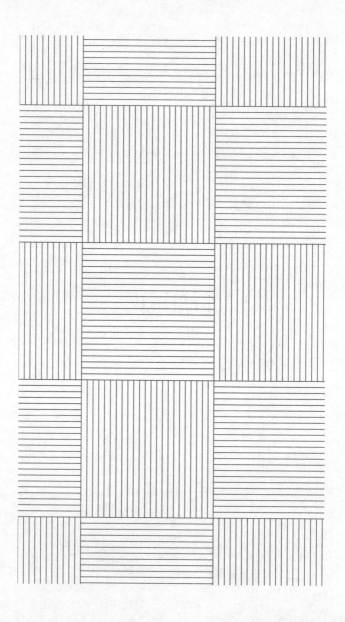

One day, *now* will be a long time ago.

———

Build your shrine at the top of a long, steep path:
A view is more beautiful when we've earned it.

———

The days are long, but the years are short.

FACING THE
PERPLEXITIES OF
RELATIONSHIPS

Ancient philosophers and contemporary scientists agree that a key—perhaps *the* key—to happiness is strong relationships with other people.

We need enduring, intimate bonds; we need to feel like we belong; we need to be able to confide; we need to be able to get and give support.

Because relationships are so essential to a happy life, any choice that deepens or broadens relationships tends to make us happier.

As we find our place among others, we have to recognize that people may hold different preferences, need different strategies, and express different perspectives from our own. When we don't understand how people can be different, we can feel hurt, puzzled, resentful, or angry that they don't see things our way. Or we can feel discouraged or frustrated with ourselves, when we can't do things someone else's way. With self-knowledge, we gain compassion for others—and also for ourselves.

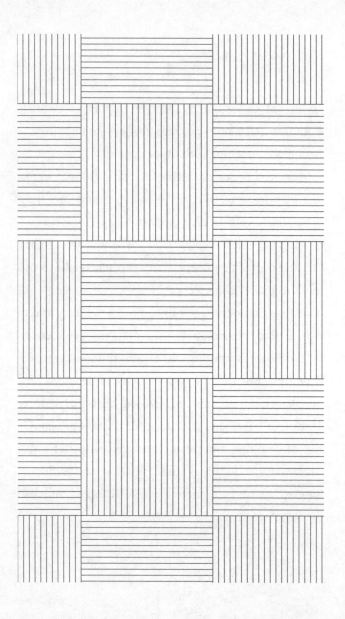

THE CHALLENGE
OF LOVE

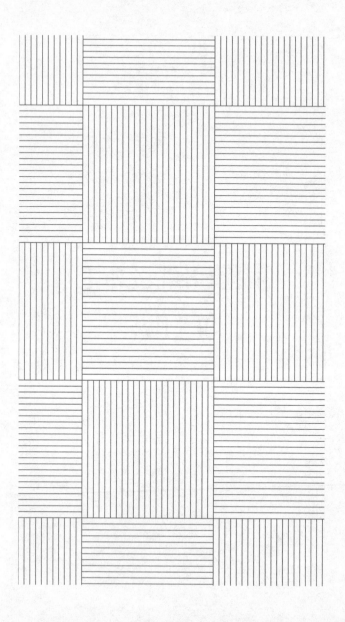

Love is unconditional, and love is demanding.

Singer-songwriter Rosanne Cash tells the story of a time she was in Nashville with her husband and professional collaborator, the producer and musician John Leventhal. Rosanne did a guest session on another band's album; John came to the recording. After the session, he didn't say anything about her performance, so Rosanne asked, "How did you like it?"

He answered, "I would have pushed you harder."

Love says, "You're the best," and love says, "You can do better." Love accepts you just as you are, and love expects the best from you.

———

We make people happier by acknowledging that they're not feeling happy.

When someone is feeling bad, we want to help them feel better. One strategy that's popular—but not very effective—is to deny their feelings. "It can't really be so bad." "This will pass in no time."

In fact, it's far more effective to acknowledge that someone is feeling bad. When we say, "That must be frightening" or "It sounds like a really frustrating experience," we help them to feel understood.

———

We care for many people we don't particularly care for.

———

We can't change our children's natures by nagging them or signing them up for classes.

———

In families, we meet people we'd never otherwise encounter.

———

Intellectual engagement can be more exciting than emotional engagement, yet these aren't the people whom we yearn for on our deathbeds.

———

At some point, a parent must shift from coach to cheer-leader.

———

Sartre wrote, "Hell is—other people!" True. And Heaven is—other people.

———

One way to thwart a conversation is to refuse to answer. Another way is to talk and talk.

———

We can't make people change. But when we change, our relationships change—and so others may also change.

———

Easy children raise good parents.

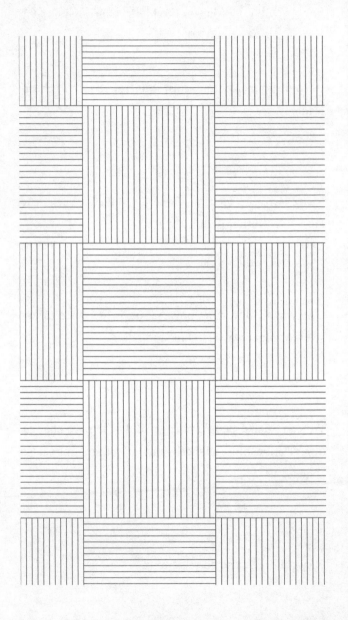

FRIENDSHIP

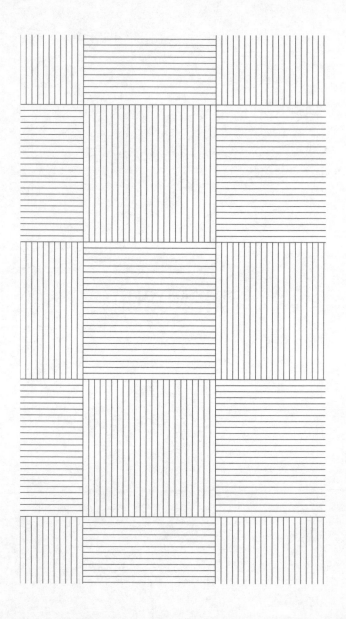

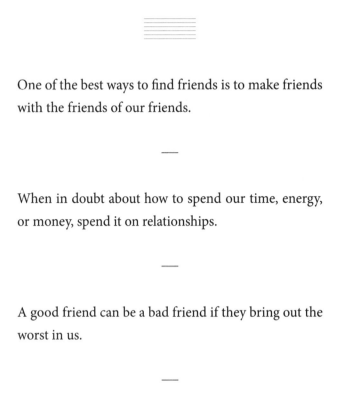

One of the best ways to find friends is to make friends with the friends of our friends.

———

When in doubt about how to spend our time, energy, or money, spend it on relationships.

———

A good friend can be a bad friend if they bring out the worst in us.

———

Working together often builds friendships faster than having fun together.

———

More friends, more safety.

—

We know what matters to people when they repeat themselves.

—

It's better to invite friends over for takeout than not to invite friends over for a home-cooked meal.

—

Sometimes we choose to confess our deepest secret to a stranger rather than a friend.

—

A young child—or better yet, a friendly dog—makes conversation easier, by smoothing over awkward pauses or supplying an excuse to change the subject.

FITTING IN
AND
STANDING OUT

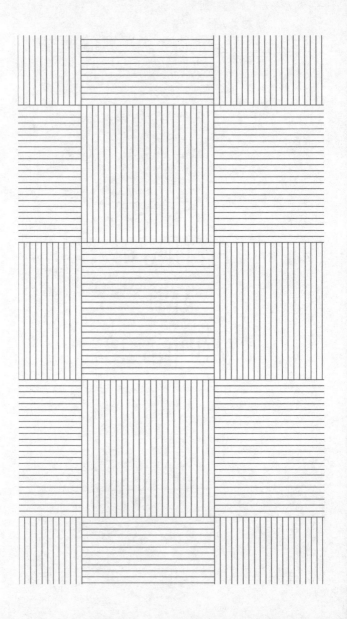

When we feel as though we don't fit in, we fit right in.

One of the most universal emotions is the feeling that we don't belong. At one point, drummer Ringo Starr briefly left the Beatles. He visited John Lennon and said, "I'm leaving the group because I'm not playing well and I feel unloved . . . and you three are really close." John said, "I thought it was *you three*!" Then Ringo visited Paul McCartney and said, "I'm leaving the band. I feel you three guys are really close and I'm out of it." Paul replied, "I thought it was *you three*!" Ringo didn't even bother to visit George Harrison.

—

Every strength contains its weakness, and weakness can bring strengths.

—

Learning when, how, and if we wish to conform is one of the most important achievements of childhood.

—

We're more like other people than we may imagine.

Because everyone goes to the grocery store on the Tuesday before Thanksgiving to beat the crowds on Wednesday, the busiest day is Tuesday. Because people visiting a public bathroom assume that the stall closest to the door gets the most use, the center stalls are most popular. We think we're outwitting others, and they try to outwit us in exactly the same way.

—

You're unique, just like everyone else.

—

Many people won't have an opinion until someone else has an opinion.

—

A strong voice repels as well as attracts.

—

Approval from the people we love and admire may be gratifying, but it's not enough to be the foundation of a happy life.

—

If we want to stand out, it helps to know how to fit in.

—

To respect us, people must first notice us; we can't earn trust and admiration from the sidelines.

—

Being a spectator is different from being a participant. Compare a visit to a zoo and a visit to a petting zoo.

—

Holding a microphone makes you feel like an expert.

—

We can be the center of a group without being its leader, and we can be a focus of attention without being a focus of interest.

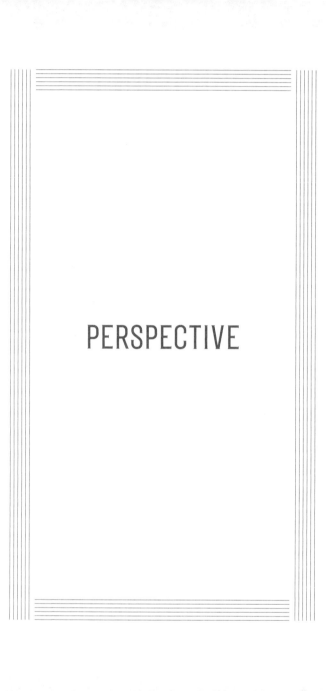

PERSPECTIVE

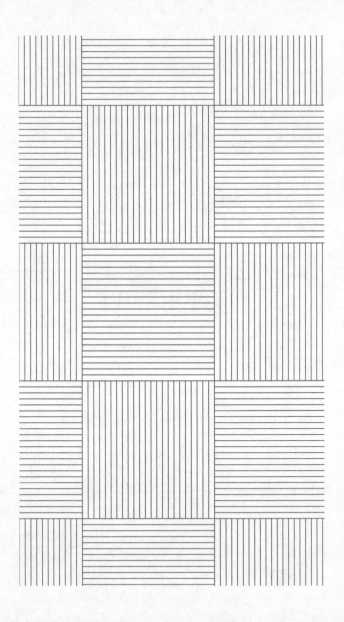

What we believe is most important isn't always what becomes most important.

When the first Roman emperor, Caesar Augustus, died, he'd nearly doubled the size of the empire, defeated Mark Antony and Cleopatra of Egypt, streamlined administration, increased trade, funded numerous construction projects, and fostered the arts. The most significant historical event during his reign was . . . the birth of Jesus.

In the sixteenth century, when Spanish explorer-soldier Francisco Pizarro seized immense treasures from South America, the most valuable thing he brought home was . . . the potato.

The First World War was one of the deadliest world conflicts in history. It spurred technological advances in the use of warplanes, submarines, machine guns, artillery, tanks, and poison gas that led to carnage on a massive scale. The war killed less than a third as many people as . . . the flu.

Many successful and respected artists, such as J. M. Barrie, Hans Christian Andersen, E. B. White, Frances

Hodgson Burnett, Robert Louis Stevenson, C. S. Lewis, and Rudyard Kipling are best remembered for the works they created . . . for children.

———

What we see depends on where we stand.

In an old joke, a traveler is standing beside a river and desperate to cross. He sees a man fishing on the far bank, and shouts, "Quick, tell me, how do I get to the other side?" The man looks puzzled. So the traveler yells again, "Tell me, how do I get to the other side of the river?" And the man answers, "Mister, you *are* on the other side of the river."

In a park, a little girl was talking animatedly to a squirrel. A passerby kindly said to her, "Oh, honey, I don't think that squirrel speaks Spanish."

———

I admire nature, and I am also nature. I resent traffic, and I am also traffic.

———

We can hurt people when we try to force them to fit into our framework.

In Greek mythology, the cruel Procrustes would invite travelers to spend the night. No visitors fit his special iron bed exactly, so to make them fit, he'd stretch their bodies or amputate their limbs.

Likewise, it's tempting to assume that if a habit makes one person happy, it will suit someone else just as well—but often it does not.

No bed fits every traveler, and there's no single, standard solution to happiness or good habits.

—

We may judge others harshly for actions that we're engaging in ourselves, or we may contribute to the very conditions we deplore. The tourist complains, "All these awful tourists are ruining this place," or the minimalist announces, "Embrace the value of simple living with my extensive line of branded merchandise," or the committee head explains, "The important mission of the Work/Life Balance Task Force will require you to stay late several evenings each month."

—

It's easier to notice the exceptional than the familiar, so to observe the obvious requires intense attention.

—

Sometimes fewer words allow us to convey more.

During the Second World War, General Dwight Eisenhower needed to inform the combined chiefs of staff of Germany's unconditional surrender. Eisenhower's colleagues proposed various grand statements for the triumphant victory message. Eisenhower rejected all suggestions and wrote:

> *The mission of this Allied Force was fulfilled at 0241, local time, May 7th, 1945.*
>
> *EISENHOWER*

No magniloquence could match the power of that simple statement.

—

Before declaring that something is superficial, un-healthy, inefficient, dangerous, disgusting, or immoral, we should consider: *Maybe this just doesn't suit my taste.*

—

Words matter, metaphors matter.

In 1488, King John II of Portugal rebranded South Africa's aptly named "Cape of Storms" as the "Cape of Good Hope" to encourage trade. During the Second World War, Winston Churchill suggested the name "Mosquito Fleet" for a fleet of fast, small craft, then bettered it to "Hornet Fleet," then again to "Shark Fleet." As the times changed, an agricultural group changed the term from "prunes" to "dried plums" and back to "prunes" again. Consider:

- Do you play the piano or practice the piano?
- Are you networking or engaging with co-workers?

- Is that room in your house an office, a study, or a library?
- Are you lowering your standards or lowering the bar?
- Do you spend time or invest time?
- Are you the one who has been singled out or the one who has been chosen?
- Do you think about office politics or office diplomacy?
- Are you getting your daily exercise, going for a run, or training for the marathon?
- Are you taking a ditch day or personal day or mental-health day?
- Do you have to do it or do you get to do it?

By changing our words, we can change our perspective.

MAKING
THINGS
HAPPEN

Years ago, when I was a lawyer, I clerked for Supreme Court Justice Sandra Day O'Connor, which was one of those extraordinary, once-in-a-lifetime work experiences.

One day, when I was telling her about a book I was writing about happiness, she said, "I can tell you what *I* believe is the secret to a happy life."

"What's that, Justice?" I asked.

"Work worth doing."

"Interesting, but isn't that somewhat . . . limited?"

"No," she said firmly. "Work worth doing. That's all you really need."

The more I've thought about her answer, the more I realize its brilliance. Because, of course, "work" can mean so many different things; to do work that's "worth doing" means that we must choose work that reflects our values. And we have many kinds of work: work-work, home-work, relationships-work, community-work, self-work.

Whatever kind of work we're doing, though, we want to be able to make things happen. We need to be able to plan, persist, and act effectively, with a sense of purpose. We need to be able to have an idea—and carry it out.

Also, we must find the approach that's *right for us*. To get things done, one person thrives with plenty of accountability; another needs a week-to-week plan; another works best with spontaneity and freedom.

By understanding ourselves—and also understanding how other people might be different from us—we can make choices and take actions that allow us to build the lives we want.

WORK

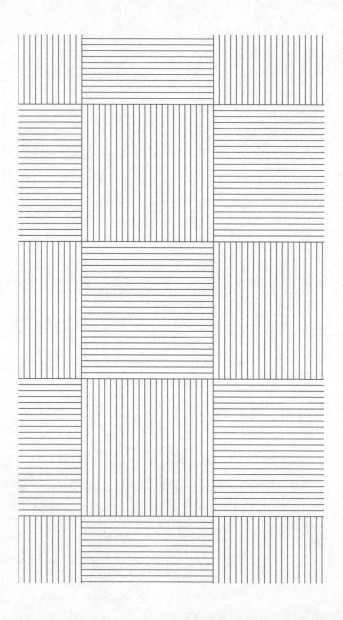

The best kind of work is the work you would do for fun and for free.

Basketball superstar Michael Jordan insisted on the inclusion of an unusual clause in his contract. Teams routinely forbid their valuable players from taking unnecessary risks, but Jordan's contract with the Chicago Bulls allowed him to play any basketball he wanted—an exhibition game, a demonstration, a pickup game, or a scrimmage—for the "love of the game."

For the love of the game!

—

The person who works the hardest isn't necessarily doing the best work.

Celebrated actors Laurence Olivier and Dustin Hoffman worked together on the 1976 film *Marathon Man*. Supposedly, when Hoffman told Olivier that to prepare for a scene where his character had been awake for three days, he hadn't slept for forty-eight hours, Olivier replied, "My dear boy, why don't you just try acting?"

———

As Jean Piaget, Maria Montessori, and Fred Rogers observed: Play is the work of childhood. And at its best, work is the play of adulthood.

In her autobiography, Agatha Christie writes that as a child, she played make-believe with her imaginary "Kittens." She would sit at her old nurse's feet and murmur to herself, playing secret games with Clover, Blackie, Mrs. Benson, and all the others.

Many years later, her sister challenged her to write a detective story. Christie recalled that one day, after she spotted a man and two women on a tram, "I took them all three off the tram with me to work upon—and walked up Barton Road muttering to myself just as in the days of the Kittens." This story became her first published novel, *The Mysterious Affair at Styles*, and introduced her celebrated character Inspector Poirot.

Work is the play of adulthood.

———

If we're not failing, we're not trying hard enough.

—

A short putt may seem easier than a long drive, but the golfer who focuses only on showy efforts will lose the round.

—

Beautiful tools make work a joy.

—

Where we start out makes a big difference in where we end up.

—

More trial, more error—and more accomplishment.

—

Luck plays an enormous role in success, and hard work is a way to attract luck.

—

It's easy to assume that accomplishing a difficult task would be easier at a different moment: "Before I had kids." "Next summer." "Ten years ago." In 1512, after completing the Sistine Chapel, Michelangelo wrote to his father:

> I have finished the chapel I was painting: the pope is very happy with it, but other things haven't turned out as well as I hoped. I blame the times, which are so unfavorable to our art.

Michelangelo was then living in the middle of the High Renaissance, a period that's considered a pinnacle in the history of Western art.

When we're doing something hard, it feels like the times are hard.

RESPONSIBILITY

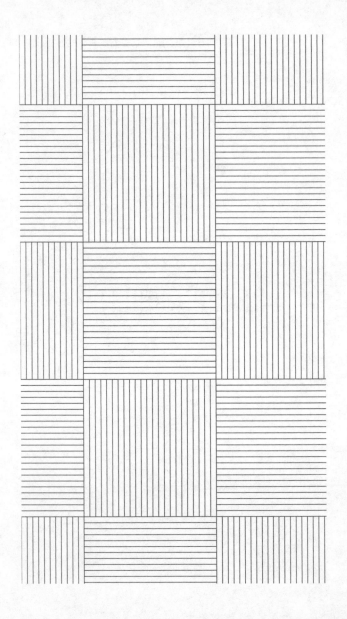

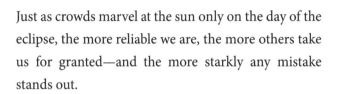

Just as crowds marvel at the sun only on the day of the eclipse, the more reliable we are, the more others take us for granted—and the more starkly any mistake stands out.

—

It can be more difficult to be the mind that directs than the hand that executes.

—

The sharing of tasks often leads to the shirking of tasks.

—

If we can't be loving, we can be kind; if we can't be kind, we can be courteous; if we can't be courteous, we can be quiet.

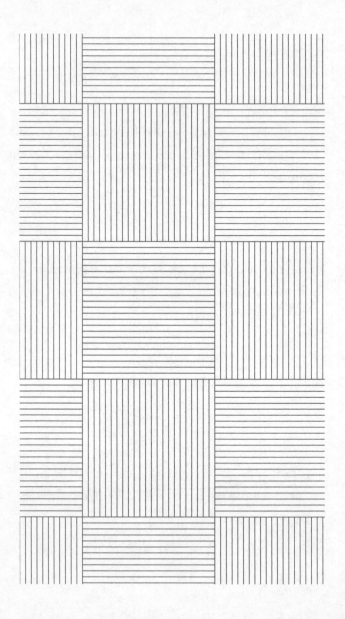

THE THIRST FOR
KNOWLEDGE

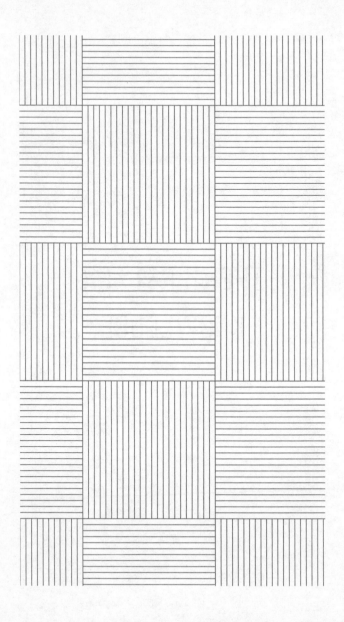

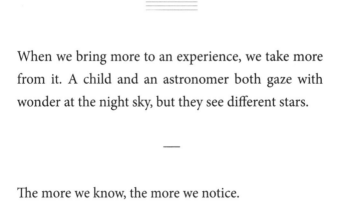

When we bring more to an experience, we take more from it. A child and an astronomer both gaze with wonder at the night sky, but they see different stars.

—

The more we know, the more we notice.

—

People love to learn, and they also love to teach and share.

—

Selection matters. We can't make sense of a textbook in which every sentence is underlined.

—

The opposite of a profound truth is also true.

—

More knowledge, more questions.

—

One quality of a great artistic or scientific work is that it inspires other great artistic or scientific works.

CREATIVITY

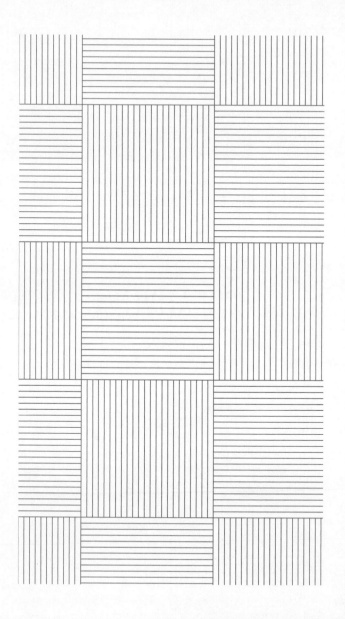

To make something beautiful, it's often necessary to add a touch of ugly. Beautiful music often features notes of dissonance. A lovely fragrance often incorporates some bad smells. An elegant living room includes a garish green pillow. A hint of sour deepens flavors.

—

To generate new ideas, embrace new tools. The introduction of paint in tubes stimulated the Impressionist movement; advances in organic chemistry led to blockbuster perfumes like Chanel No. 5 and CK One; the Roland TR-808 drum machine helped inspire hip-hop.

—

Pouring out ideas is better for the imagination than doling them out by the teaspoon.

———

If we're not likely to win a starring role, we can stage our own performance.

———

Flawed can be more perfect than perfection. An accomplished juggler will deliberately drop a prop.

———

Putting materials into our hands often puts ideas into our heads.

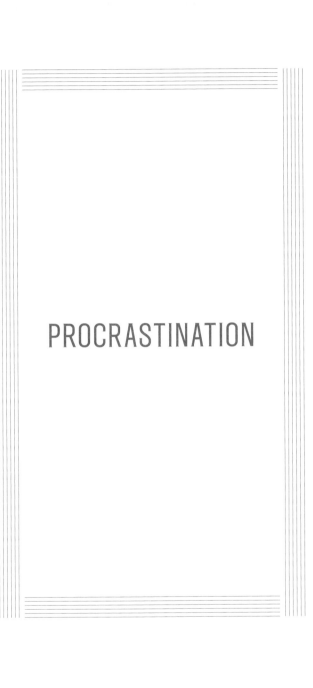

PROCRASTINATION

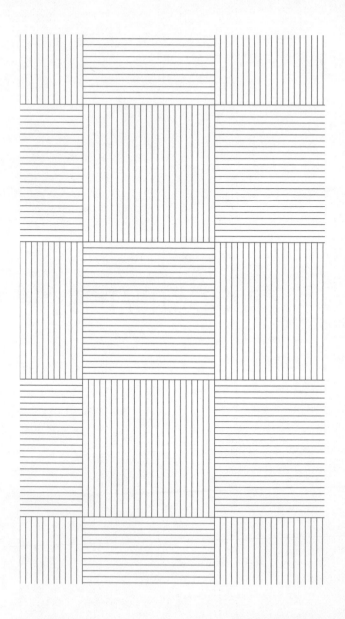

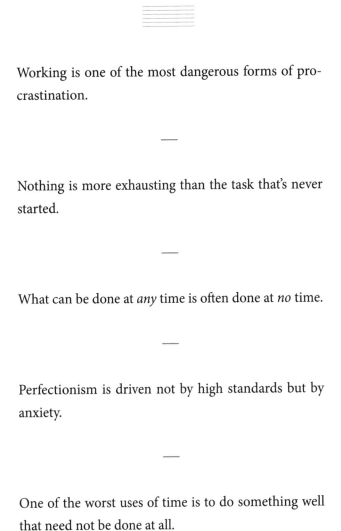

Working is one of the most dangerous forms of procrastination.

———

Nothing is more exhausting than the task that's never started.

———

What can be done at *any* time is often done at *no* time.

———

Perfectionism is driven not by high standards but by anxiety.

———

One of the worst uses of time is to do something well that need not be done at all.

—

Do you need more time, or do you need to make a decision?

—

We often justify procrastination with questionable assumptions: "I can't do creative work in the afternoon," "I'll do better if I begin in the new year," "Unless I have three hours free from interruption, it's not worth trying to get anything done."

HOUSEKEEPING

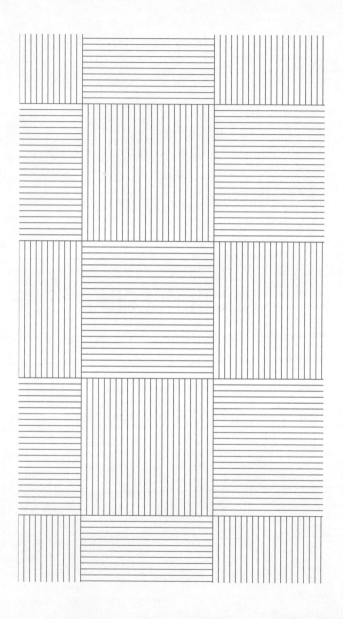

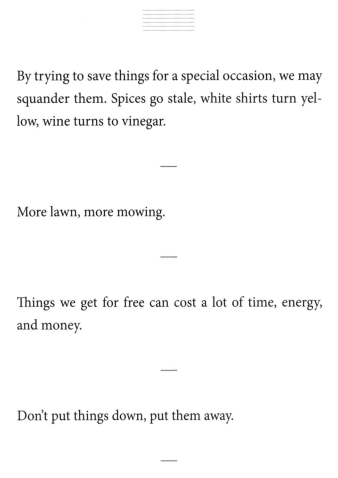

By trying to save things for a special occasion, we may squander them. Spices go stale, white shirts turn yellow, wine turns to vinegar.

———

More lawn, more mowing.

———

Things we get for free can cost a lot of time, energy, and money.

———

Don't put things down, put them away.

———

Outer order can contribute to inner calm.

—

Someplace, keep an empty shelf; someplace, keep a junk drawer.

—

If you don't like a pair of pants, don't pay to get them hemmed.

TAKING ACTION

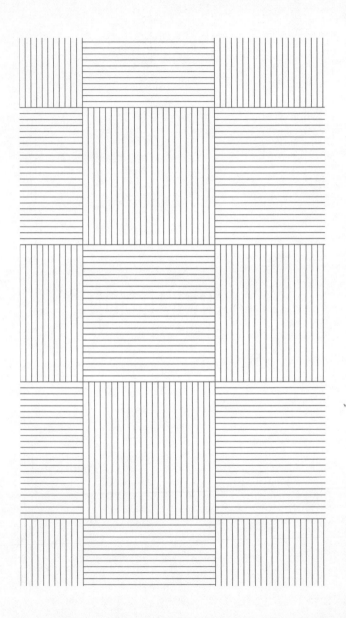

We often change what's easy to change, rather than what needs to change.

At times, we feel the need for transformation but tackle the wrong aspect of our lives.

Some people get an executive coach when they need a therapist, or get a therapist when they really need a coach.

They give up coffee rather than give up wine.

They renovate their kitchen instead of fixing their marriage (then argue about countertops and get divorced).

They try to fix someone else rather than addressing their own problems.

A woman told her real-estate broker that she no longer wanted to move, because, she explained, "I thought I wanted an apartment with outdoor space, but I realized that I really want a husband."

—

Telling people what to do is a very different skill from doing it ourselves. Mediocre writers can be great editors, and unprincipled gurus can lead others to enlightenment.

———

In life as in battle, when advancing, it's hard to start; when retreating, it's hard to stop. It's hard to pick up a book, and it's hard to put it down unfinished.

———

The easiest time to get onto a tennis court is when a big match is being televised.

———

No tool fits every hand.

———

Slicing is easier than ripping.

———

The god of shipwreck is also the god of windfall.

———

Seeds have no power to move, yet through ingenious design, they can travel enormous distances.

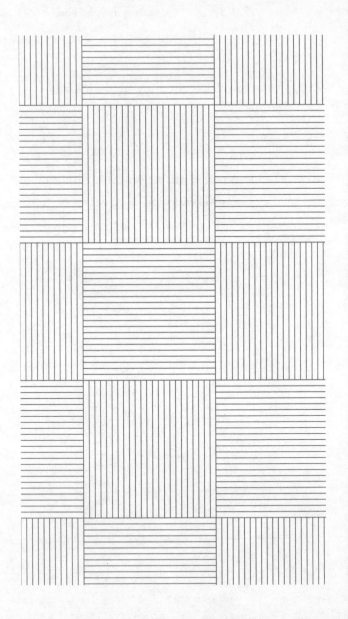

PERSISTENCE

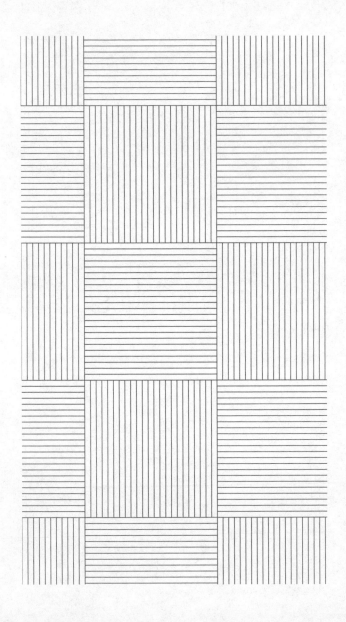

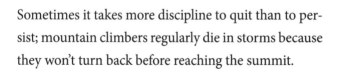

Sometimes it takes more discipline to quit than to persist; mountain climbers regularly die in storms because they won't turn back before reaching the summit.

—

Although we go the same distance, the design of a staircase can make the climb easier or harder.

—

Sometimes, to keep going, we need to allow ourselves to stop.

—

We can find our courage from someone else's fear.

—

We can ask more from ourselves when we give more to ourselves.

—

Realizing that we're not suited to a certain type of work doesn't make us a failure.

—

We don't have to be good at something to be good at something. Dolly Parton, Michael Jackson, and Paul McCartney never learned to read music.

CONFRONTING
LIFE'S
DILEMMAS

Over and over, as we go through life, we must grapple with aims that are in tension—conflicts that can never truly be resolved.

We want to embrace the moment, and also prepare for the future.

We want to stay open to new ideas and to criticism, and also remain committed to our own vision.

We want to avoid mistakes and regret, and also embrace risks.

We want to show consideration for others, and also respect our own needs and desires.

We want to make our decisions thoughtfully, and also seize opportunities and avoid analysis-paralysis.

We want to learn and improve, and also let go of goals that aren't right for us.

With time and experience, we get better at facing these kinds of dilemmas, but unfortunately, they rarely become easier. That's because to find our way forward, we must manage competing desires, we must accept the compromises and stress that come from making choices, we must say "no" to ourselves—again and again and again.

One of the biggest decisions I ever made was to switch careers from law to writing. That choice became clear the moment I realized, "At this point, I'd rather fail as a writer than succeed as a lawyer."

Benjamin Franklin observed, "Experience keeps a dear school, yet Fools will learn in no other." Sometimes the right Secret of Adulthood can be the teacher who helps us learn a hard lesson without paying a high price.

TOUGH DECISIONS

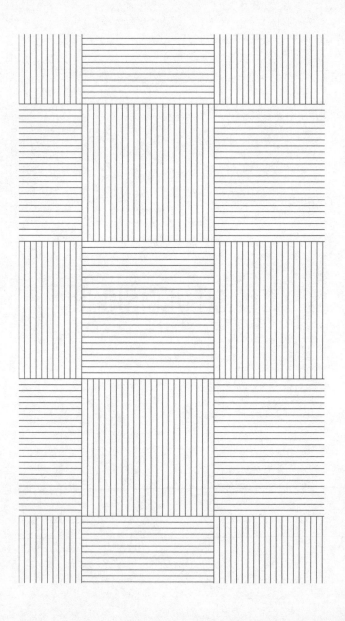

With some questions, the very inclination to consider the question suggests the answer.

For instance, for these questions, the answer is probably "Yes": "Am I a decent parent?" "Do I have a drinking problem?" "Am I carrying too much, should I take two trips?" "Should I bring an umbrella?" "Should I finally get a dog?"

But for other questions—such as "Are these ingredients healthy?" "Should I stay up late to watch one more episode?" "Should I hit 'send' on this angry email?"—the answer is probably "No."

—

Experience is a great teacher, but make sure that you're not learning the wrong lesson.

In Aesop's famous fable, the Hare challenged the Tortoise to a race. The Tortoise agreed, they set the course, and at the signal, they both started off. The Hare bounded ahead, but because he was so sure of winning, he stopped to take a nap. Meanwhile, the Tortoise plodded on. The Hare woke with a start just as the Tortoise was crossing the finish line.

The traditional moral of the fable is "Slow and steady wins the race." But wouldn't a more fitting moral be "Those with great gifts can be defeated by their own arrogance and idleness"? Or "Overconfidence fosters carelessness"? Or, as Marie von Ebner-Eschenbach wrote, "Since its famous victory over the hare, the tortoise thinks it's a sprinter"—in other words, it's easy to attribute a victory to our own abilities, when in fact we won due to circumstances or someone else's mistake.

Wisdom comes from discerning the truest lesson from an experience.

———

Choices are challenging: Packing to leave is much harder than packing to return.

———

It's easier to enforce rules than to be fair.

—

If the trash cans are overflowing, we can empty the trash more often, or we can add more trash cans, or we can remove the trash cans altogether.

—

Whenever we choose one path, we must forgo other paths, so any choice may bring unavoidable regret.

—

We often know that we want to leave before we know where we want to go.

—

Decisions will be made, by choice or by chance, because not deciding is a decision. Not choosing is a choice.

—

It's more fun to change the wallpaper than to fix the roof, but it's less important.

—

Many decisions are difficult because the choices are so similar; when neither is clearly the right choice, maybe neither is the wrong choice.

—

We resist change, so if you're thinking about making a change, you probably should have made that change months ago.

—

When a decision matters a great deal to someone else, but doesn't matter much to you, let them have their way.

—

Don't judge the wisdom of a decision by its outcome.

—

When uncertain about how to proceed, make the choice that allows you to . . .

- Choose the bigger life
- Step into the future
- Live in an atmosphere of growth
- Deepen or broaden your relationships
- Put your values into the world

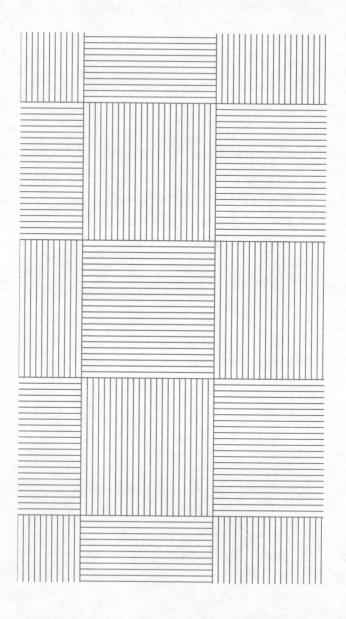

TEMPTATIONS

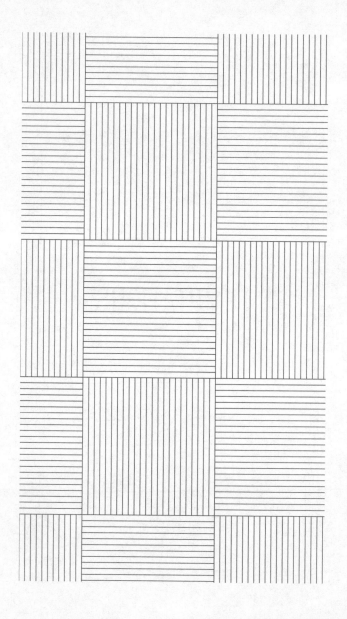

More roads, more traffic.

As New York City grew, its traffic grew, so urban planner Robert Moses built more roads. But in a counterintuitive phenomenon called "induced demand," as more roads were added, more people drove their cars—so the city's traffic got worse.

This phenomenon is literally true, and it also suggests a deeper truth. Often, when we give ourselves more of what we crave, we don't feel satisfied; we want even *more*.

—

Petty, immediate pleasures may crowd out great and enduring pleasures.

—

With a strong temptation, we often must give it up, or give up to it.

—

By giving something up, we may gain. Briefly depriving ourselves of a pleasure often has one of two good
results: either it reawakens our enjoyment or reveals
that we're happier when we don't indulge.

—

The forbidden pleasures of childhood often become
the luxuries of adulthood: buying hardback books, eat-
ing sugary cereal, playing video games, staying up late.

—

Nothing is stronger than a weakness.

—

One of the best uses of willpower is to avoid situations
that require willpower.

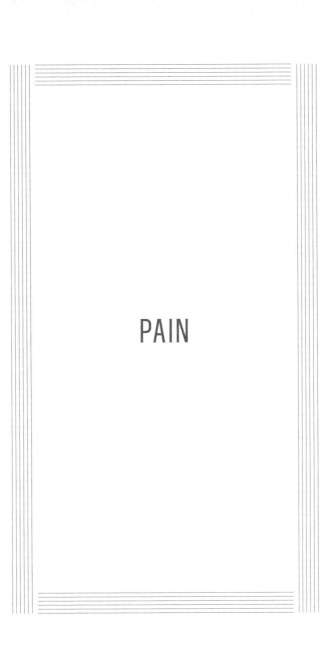

PAIN

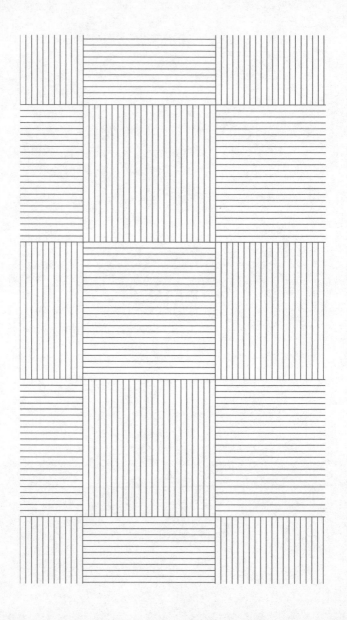

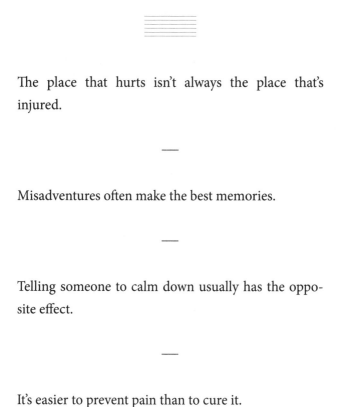

The place that hurts isn't always the place that's injured.

—

Misadventures often make the best memories.

—

Telling someone to calm down usually has the opposite effect.

—

It's easier to prevent pain than to cure it.

—

Every medicine can become poison.

—

Repeatedly rehearsing disaster doesn't protect us from it.

—

More people will line up to tour a Poison Garden than an Apothecary Garden.

DESIRE

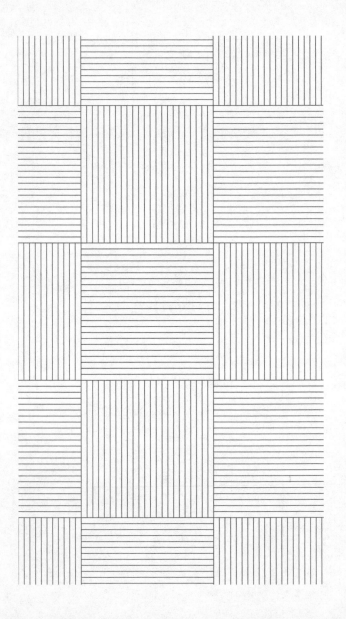

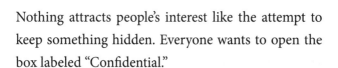

Nothing attracts people's interest like the attempt to keep something hidden. Everyone wants to open the box labeled "Confidential."

—

We don't yearn for what's distant; we want the things that seem just out of reach.

—

It can be useful to have two projects going, or romantic crushes on two people; having two saves us from getting overinvested.

—

An almond tastes better when we eat just one.

—

If we don't really want something, getting it won't make us happy.

———

Enthusiasm is a form of social courage.

———

Abstinence can be easier than moderation.

———

We can choose what we *do*, but we can't choose what we *like* to do.

GETTING IT WRONG

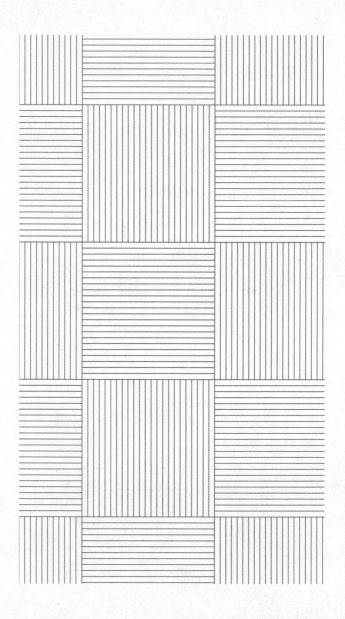

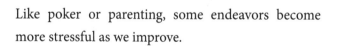

Like poker or parenting, some endeavors become more stressful as we improve.

—

Don't confuse a fire drill with a fire.

—

We can be wrong for a very long time without noticing. Bloodletting was a common medical treatment for two millennia.

—

The person who knows the most facts doesn't always have the best judgment.

—

Arguing about definitions is like drinking salt water. The more we do it, the less satisfied we feel.

—

None of us can escape our time. Scientific genius Isaac Newton wrote more than a million words on alchemy.

CONSEQUENCES

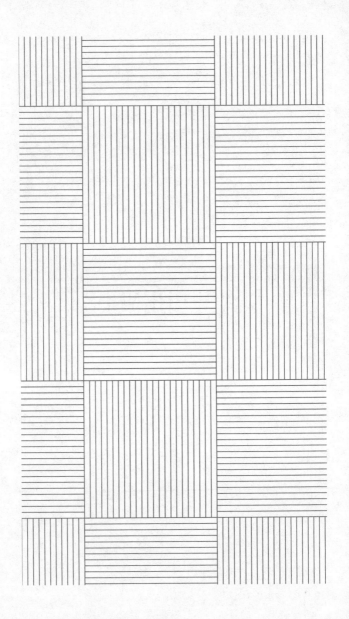

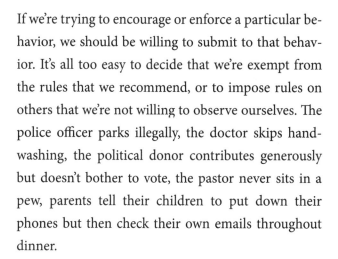

If we're trying to encourage or enforce a particular behavior, we should be willing to submit to that behavior. It's all too easy to decide that we're exempt from the rules that we recommend, or to impose rules on others that we're not willing to observe ourselves. The police officer parks illegally, the doctor skips handwashing, the political donor contributes generously but doesn't bother to vote, the pastor never sits in a pew, parents tell their children to put down their phones but then check their own emails throughout dinner.

—

If we take the credit, we must accept the blame.

—

If we take the blame when we deserve it, people will give us responsibility.

—

Solicitude, even when heartfelt, can be tiring.

—

Sometimes situations can be safer when they seem less safe. Because traffic circles feel more hazardous, drivers take greater care and, for that reason, traffic circles are safer than signal-light intersections.

—

We all want to cast our own dice.

SIMPLE SECRETS
OF ADULTHOOD

When facing the difficulties of adulthood, sometimes we need to reflect on timeless truths—and sometimes we just need practical advice.

Concrete and manageable, these minor Secrets of Adulthood solve common problems and give immediate results. They're also simple enough to be memorable: When I remind myself, "If I can't find something, search *very thoroughly* in the place where I'd expect it to be," my missing item usually turns up within ten minutes.

Over and over, I've been astonished by how a small step can provide a big benefit. Without demanding much time, energy, or money, these hacks can make our daily lives much easier.

- If you don't know what to do with yourself, go outside or go to sleep.
- Every to-do list should include one item that can be crossed off in the first five minutes.
- Present information in threes.
- It's okay to ask for help.

- If you're dreading a family occasion, bring a guest. Many difficult people behave better in front of outsiders.
- If you forgot you owned an item, you can probably get rid of it.
- Turning something on and off a few times often fixes a glitch.
- Sometimes it's easier to make last-minute plans than to plan in advance.
- Even a weekend away from home and routine can be enough for a real vacation.
- One way to answer a difficult question is strategically to misunderstand it.
- People probably aren't as interested in your hobby or your travels as they seem to be.
- Don't buy things until you need them: Store them at the store.
- If you can't find an item, search *very thoroughly* in the place where you'd expect that item to be.
- Leave some room in the suitcase.
- Focus on actions, not outcomes. (Don't try to "learn to play the guitar"; instead, "play the guitar for twenty minutes daily.")

- Don't wait until you have more free time. You may never have more free time.
- Cheerfulness is contagious, and crabbiness is even more contagious.
- To fall asleep faster, make sure your feet are warm.
- Things look better when arranged on a tray.
- If there's something you want to do, make it more convenient; if there's something you want to resist doing, make it less convenient.
- To get a quick burst of energy, do ten jumping jacks.
- Don't let yourself fall into "empty": Keep gas in your car, stash snacks in your bag, charge your phone.
- Whenever you leave your seat, look back to make sure you haven't left anything behind.
- It's easier to see what's present than what's absent.
- Things often get messier before they get tidier.
- Keep mementos that are small in size and few in number.

- Try by age twenty-five: Many lifelong preferences are set by young adulthood, so try new things when you're young.
- Before accepting an invitation for the future, imagine that you must show up tonight.
- If possible, have a challenging conversation while walking.
- Beware of "procrasti-clearing"—cleaning or organizing as an excuse to delay work.
- To understand a new place, visit a grocery store.
- Don't do something to make yourself feel *better* if it just ends up making you feel *worse*.
- If you're not sure how to have fun, ask yourself, "What did I do for fun when I was ten years old?"
- Once a group includes five people, a single conversation is very hard to maintain.
- If you're buying an item that you're not sure you'll use, buy or borrow a cheap one (yoga mat, kitchen knife, tennis racket), and then if you use it regularly, upgrade.
- When packing an item that might leak, put it in a plastic bag.

- Taking advice signals affection or respect: When someone recommends a book, read it; when a person recommends a TV show, watch it.
- To quiet a crowd, blow on a harmonica.
- If you're nervous about an upcoming event or experience, visit the location ahead of time to make it more familiar.
- Most decisions don't require extensive research.
- By doing a little each day, you can accomplish a lot.
- In a new place, we have special energy, so unpack everything as soon as you move in, and push yourself hard when you take a new hike.
- When teaching information or telling a story, highlight what's interesting to the audience, not what's fun for you to discuss.
- Follow the one-minute rule: If you can do a task in less than one minute, do it without delay.
- If you can't think of a topic of conversation, ask, "What's keeping you busy these days?"
- If someone might not remember your name, re-introduce yourself.
- If you can't find something, clean up.

YOUR SECRETS
OF ADULTHOOD

ACKNOWLEDGMENTS

What a joy it was to write *Secrets of Adulthood*! I've been collecting aphorisms for practically my whole life and writing my own aphorisms for a few decades; gathering my favorite examples into one book has been such a happy project.

I have so many people to thank.

Thanks, first, to the readers, podcast listeners, booksellers, and librarians. I so appreciate your enthusiasm and support.

So many people help me put my words out into the world.

Thanks once again to my outstanding agent, Christy Fletcher, for all her invaluable guidance, as well as to Melissa Chinchillo and Yona Levin of UTA, and to Victoria Hobbs.

Thanks to my editor, Gillian Blake, for her acumen and skill, and also to the terrific Crown team: Julie

Cepler, David Drake, Amy Li, Annsley Rosner, Gwyneth Stansfield, Kimberly Lew, Dyana Messina, Christopher Brand, and Andrea Lau.

Thanks to Alice Truax, for her incisive editorial suggestions.

I feel very lucky to get to work with the extraordinary team of Gretchen Rubin Media: Anne Mercogliano and Adam Caswell, Annie Jolley, Emy Joyeux, Jason Konrad, Lindsay Logan, Molly Weissman, Jenna Williams, and Hannah Wilson. Working with you makes me happy every day.

Thanks to the people who work with me on the *Happier with Gretchen Rubin* podcast: my co-host and sister Elizabeth Craft, Chuck Reed and everyone at Audacy, and Ben Davis at WME.

Last of all, once again, thanks to all the members of my family and my friends, who in some cases have helped to inspire these aphorisms, and certainly have endured hearing me repeat them many times.

NOTES

Big Ideas in a Few Words

14 **"You can sink so fast"** Marie von Ebner-Eschenbach, *Aphorisms* (New York: Ariadne Press, 1994).

14 **"It is much easier"** François de La Rochefoucauld, *Collected Maxims and Other Reflections* (New York: Oxford University Press, 2008).

14 **"All severity that does not tend"** James Boswell, *The Life of Samuel Johnson* (New York: Penguin Classics, 2008).

14 **"Curiosity is not the same"** Iris Murdoch, *The Flight from the Enchanter* (New York: Viking, 1956).

14 **"Nobody really looks"** Kenneth Goldsmith, ed., *I'll Be Your Mirror: The Selected Andy Warhol Interviews* (New York: Carroll & Graf, 2004).

14 **"Failure is good preparation"** Sarah Manguso, *300 Arguments: Essays* (New York: Graywolf, 2017).

14 **"To be really happy"** Winston Churchill, *Painting as a Pastime* (New York: Cornerstone, 1965).

15 **"No man is happy"** Publius Syrus, *The Moral Sayings* (Cleveland: L. E. Barnard, 1856).

15 **"There are men who"** Luc de Clapiers, marquis of Vauvenargues, *Reflections and Maxims* (London: Humphrey Milford, 1940).

Cultivating Ourselves

29 **"I am depressed because"** James Agee, *Letters of James Agee to Father Flye* (New York: Bantam, 1963).

39 **"I have lied"** Michael Cohen, Testimony Before House Oversight Committee, February 27, 2019.

39 **Notorious murderer Malcolm Macarthur** Mark O'Connell, *A Thread of Violence* (New York: Doubleday, 2023).

41 **"I often paint fakes"** Arthur Koestler, *The Act of Creation* (New York: Macmillan, 1964).

Facing the Perplexities of Relationships

57 **"I would have pushed you"** Gretchen Rubin and Elizabeth Craft, hosts, *Happier with Gretchen Rubin,* podcast, "Creativity! Listen to Rosanne Cash, Save Your String, Fight Drift, and a Lesson from the Writers' Room," July 22, 2015, interview with Rosanne Cash.

59 **"Hell is—other people!"** Jean-Paul Sartre, *No Exit and Three Other Plays* (New York: Vintage, 1989).

67 **Ringo didn't even bother** The Beatles, *The Beatles Anthology* (New York: Chronicle Books, 2002).

77 **"Mosquito Fleet"** Memorandum to First Lord, First Sea Lord, and General Ismay, May 2, 1943, in Winston Churchill, *The Hinge of Fate* (Boston: Houghton Mifflin, 1950).

Making Things Happen

85 **for the "love of the game"** Jesse Dorsey, "7 Most Ridiculous Contract Clauses in NBA History," *Bleacher Report,* May 3, 2012.

85 **"My dear boy, why don't you"** Hanna Flint, "Jeremy Strong and Hollywood's Most Extreme Actors," BBC, March 22, 2023.

86   **"I took them all three"**   Agatha Christie, *An Autobiography* (New York: G. P. Putnam's Sons, 1977).

88   **"I have finished the chapel"**   Michelangelo, *Poems and Letters,* trans. Anthony Mortimer (New York: Penguin Classics, 2007).

Confronting Life's Dilemmas

122   **"Experience keeps a dear"**   Benjamin Franklin, *Poor Richard's Almanack* (New York: Skyhorse, 2007).

126   **"Since its famous victory"**   Marie von Ebner-Eschenbach, *Aphorisms* (New York: Ariadne Press, 1994).

RESOURCES

Books

Gretchen Rubin is the author of many bestselling books on happiness, habits, and human nature. She combines rigorous research with personal observation to help readers know themselves better, and become happier, healthier, more productive, and more creative.

Life in Five Senses: How Exploring the Senses Got Me Out of My Head and Into the World

Better Than Before: What I Learned About Making and Breaking Habits—to Sleep More, Quit Sugar, Procrastinate Less, and Generally Build a Happier Life

The Happiness Project: Or, Why I Spent a Year Trying to Sing in the Morning, Clean My Closets, Fight Right, Read Aristotle, and Generally Have More Fun

The Four Tendencies: The Indispensable Personality Profiles That Reveal How to Make Your Life Better (and Other People's Lives Better, Too)

Happier at Home: Kiss More, Jump More, Abandon Self-Control, and My Other Experiments in Everyday Life

Outer Order, Inner Calm: *Declutter and Organize to Make More Room for Happiness*

Podcast

Every week on *Happier with Gretchen Rubin,* Gretchen brings her practical, manageable insights about happiness and good habits to this lively, thought-provoking podcast. Gretchen's co-host is her younger sister, Elizabeth Craft, a TV writer and producer, who (lovingly) refers to Gretchen as her happiness bully. They explore a wide range of topics, from quick happiness hacks to fascinating discoveries about human nature.

Website

Explore Gretchen's articles on popular topics, discover strategies for happiness and habits, take quizzes, and download helpful resources.

Visit gretchenrubin.com.

Quizzes

We can build a happy life only on the foundation of our own nature, our own values, and our own interests—but it's surprisingly hard to know ourselves. Gretchen's quizzes will help you know yourself better, so you can create a happier, healthier, more productive, and more creative life.

Visit gretchenrubin.com/quiz.

Newsletter

Join more than one million subscribers and sign up for Gretchen's free *Five Things Making Me Happy* newsletter. Every week, you'll receive a roundup of what's making Gretchen happy, along with observations and insights into happiness and habits. You'll also receive *5 Things to Try*—a monthly collection of practical tips, hacks, and tools—and *5 Things I Published*—a monthly curation of articles, podcast episodes, and more.

Sign up at gretchenrubin.com/newsletter.

App

The Happier app is the practical toolbox to help you start your own Happiness Project and build the habits to create the life you want. Get strategies tailored specifically to you, using Gretchen Rubin's research- and observation-based principles to determine the approach that's most likely to set you up for success.

Download at thehappierapp.com, or from the Apple App Store and Google Play Store.

Webstore

On The Happiness Project store, you'll find all the practical tools, resources, and insights you need to start your own Happiness Project. There's no one-size-fits-all solution—your Happiness Project is unique to you, based on your own nature, interests, values, and experiences.

Shop now at the-happiness-project.com.

Social Media

Follow @gretchenrubin on:

ABOUT THE AUTHOR

Gretchen Rubin is one of today's most influential observers of happiness and human nature. She's the author of many books, including the blockbuster *New York Times* bestsellers *The Happiness Project, The Four Tendencies, Better Than Before,* and *Life in Five Senses.* Her books have sold more than 3.5 million copies worldwide, in more than thirty languages. She hosts the top-ranking, award-winning podcast *Happier with Gretchen Rubin,* where she explores practical solutions for living a happier life. Raised in Kansas City, she lives in New York City with her family.